REGIONAL W
NEW FO

Paul Sterry

DIAL
HOUSE

First published 1995

ISBN 0 7110 2294 1

Published by Dial House
an imprint of Ian Allan Ltd, Terminal House, Station Approach, Shepperton, Surrey TW17 8AS;
and printed by Ian Allan Printing Ltd, Coombelands House, Coombelands Lane, Addlestone, Weybridge, Surrey KT15 1HY.

Contents

INTRODUCTION

Dominating the southern half of the county of Hampshire, the New Forest is one of the largest and most easily accessible areas of forest and heath in Britain. It is the nearest thing to wilderness country that southern England has to offer and its boundaries encompass more than 35,000 hectares of land.

The extent of the New Forest may be impressive, but equally remarkable is the period over which it has survived more or less intact. The region was probably cleared and settled in the Bronze Age but, even 1,000 years ago, the layout of forests and heaths would probably have been recognisable to a visitor from the 20th century. The region is mentioned in the Domesday Book of 1086 and was established in law by William the Conqueror as a royal hunting forest.

Despite its wild and untamed appearance, the New Forest is, in effect, a man-made environment, or at the very least man-influenced. Heathlands probably became established as a result of prehistoric forest clearance, the subsequent grazing pressure preventing tree recolonisation. In the past, more so than today, the forests would have been working woodlands, with the wood being used for fuel, fencing and construction.

Today, man's influence is still felt in the New Forest in a variety of ways. There is no doubt that grazing by animals introduced by man helped shape the appearance of the region. However, the grazing pressure is so intense in some areas today that close-cropped lawns are produced and tree regeneration is effectively prevented.

Upgrading the road network has lured increasing numbers of visitors to the New Forest over the last two decades, and with them have come a new set of problems. Not least of these is the sheer pressure of numbers and resulting trampling and foot erosion; there is also the almost annual threat of maliciously-started fires which devastate the tinder-dry summer heathlands.

If wildlife interest or the prospect of peace and quiet is what draws you to the New Forest, do not be put off by the thought of hordes of fellow visitors. Surprisingly few venture away from the 'honeypot' locations, or even stray more than a few hundred yards from a car park. There are still large areas of wilderness where you can walk for a whole day without seeing another soul. If you do visit the New Forest, however, please treat the environment and its plant and animal inhabitants with respect. Remember that, although you can leave at the end of the day, this is their home and they depend upon the fragile balance of nature being maintained for their continued survival.

MAP OF THE NEW FOREST

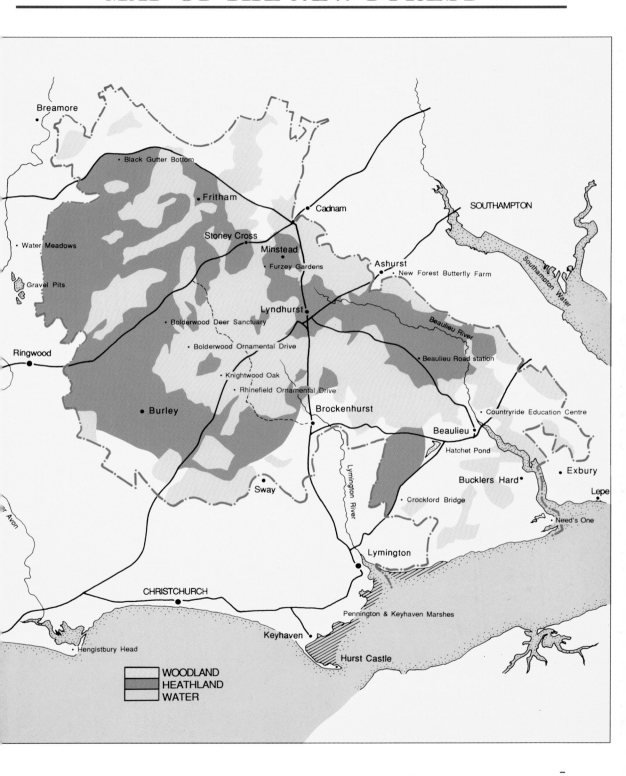

WOODLAND
HEATHLAND
WATER

Seen from the air, the New Forest is a mosaic of different habitats. It is partly this juxtaposition of niches and partly the centuries of habitat continuity that have enabled so many rich plant and animal communities to develop.
The New Forest, in its many forms, is home to almost all the plant and animal species characteristic of heaths and woodlands in southern England as a whole. In addition, it harbours a number of notable species, some of which are unique to this part of Britain.

Speak to any naturalist who knew the New Forest 20 or 30 years ago and they will confirm that the character of the region has changed, with many species in sharp decline.

Much, if not all, of the blame for this deterioration can be ascribed to overgrazing by ponies and cattle; at the very least, the problem may be one of grazing pressure in inappropriate areas, for example within inclosures, originally designed to keep stock out. It is to be hoped that an awareness of the need to conserve the New Forest's rich natural heritage will encourage a more appropriate use of the land in future.

Woodland

New Forest woodlands vary in appearance and species composition from forests of native broad-leaved trees to plantations of alien conifer species. Oak, birch and beech are typical native trees, the latter having been planted in many locations; Scots pine, Douglas fir and larch are characteristic plantation species.

Some ancient unenclosed woodlands have comparatively little understorey and are referred to as wood pastures. In the past, as today, many would have been grazed although the regimes employed were usually less intensive. In addition, a network of inclosures in the past prevented access by stock animals to many designated areas; their boundaries are often open to stock today. Where dead trees have been left standing, good habitats can be found for hole-nesting birds and invertebrates that feed on decaying wood.

In a few areas, it is possible to see evidence of other former woodland practices: some oaks and beeches show signs of pollarding where the top half of the tree has been felled creating a rounded canopy. Alders and hazels have been coppiced in some sites, the trees having been cut low to encourage a growth of thin, straight trunks.

Over the last century, conifer plantations have also appeared. By comparison with native woodlands they are impoverished from a wildlife point of view. When mature, however, they do support populations of pine hawk moths and crossbills.

Heathlands

When lowland areas with impoverished, acid soils are cleared of their natural forest cover and tree regeneration is prevented, heathland is the habitat that replaces woodland. The plant community is dominated by species such as ling and bell heather in drier areas, with cross-leaved heath, bog myrtle and sundews typical of the bogs.

The New Forest heathlands are some of the finest and most extensive areas of this fragile habitat, so threatened in other parts of southern England. It is a stronghold for birds such as Dartford warblers, hobbies and woodlarks and has unusual communities of plants, including the diminutive bog orchid.

Freshwater

Boggy flushes, pools and larger ponds are typical of the heathland habitats of the New Forest. A rich community of water bugs, beetles and aquatic plants has developed and the region is of national importance for its dragonfly and damselfly populations. These include not only good numbers of species widespread in lowland England, but also a few species more or less restricted to the New Forest. Regrettably, drainage schemes have damaged some important areas of bog in the past.

The species described and illustrated in this book have been arranged in an order which follows the convention of relevant field guides to the region.

The selection is a mixture of the most characteristic and conspicuous members of the community together with specialities of the region. Species that are likely to arouse the curiosity of the visitor have also been included.

Where appropriate, the species average length (L.) or height (H.) is given after the Latin name. Other measurements which may help identification are incorporated into the text.

BIRDS

1 Mallard *Anas platyrhynchos* (L. 56cm)
The mallard is the commonest and most widespread duck to be found in the New Forest. It occurs on all types of water, from small ponds and streams to large stretches such as Hatchet Pond. The drake has a green head and neck, and the feathers have an oily sheen. The breast is chestnut and the rest of the body is greyish-brown and finely marked. The female is mottled brown. In flight, both show a blue patch on the trailing edge of the wing. Both sexes have orange feet and variable yellowish bills. Mallards are often seen in pairs.

2 Teal *Anas crecca* (L. 36cm)
This is the smallest duck is Britain. The drake has a rich chestnut head with a dark green patch through and above the eye. The flanks are pale and covered with delicate, grey vermiculations. When seen at a distance, creamy-yellow patches on the sides of the rump are diagnostic. The female is mottle brown. In flight, both sexes show a green patch, called a speculum, on the wings. In the New Forest, teal are seen mostly on small ponds and marshy areas. They are more numerous in the winter months.

3 Buzzard *Buteo buteo* (L. 45cm)
On sunny days, the broad-winged silhouette of the buzzard is a familiar sight soaring over New Forest woodlands. Buzzards announce their presence with a loud mewing call as they soar ever higher, scanning the ground for small mammals, insects and carrion. They are sometimes mobbed by jackdaws and crows. Buzzards are brown in colour, but rather variable. The underwing is usually quite pale but with a considerable amount of dark barring. Buzzards are quite secretive when not in flight, but they are occasionally seen perched on fenceposts or dead branches in trees.

4 Kestrel *Falco tinnunculus* (L. 35cm)
The kestrel is the commonest small bird of prey to be seen in the New Forest. It is also the only species in the region that regularly hovers, often doing so above roadside verges, earning it the nickname of 'windhover'. Prey animals include small mammals, such as voles and mice, small birds and insects. The male kestrel has chestnut on the back and mantle of the wings. The head is blue-grey, as is the tail, which has a black tip. Female and immature kestrels are more uniformly mottled brown.

5 Sparrowhawk
Accipiter nisus (L. 35cm)
Sparrowhawks are fairly common in the New Forest but much more unobtrusive than kestrels. In spring, males are sometimes seen circling over woodlands. Otherwise, both sexes are seen flying low over the ground or through woodland, in pursuit of small birds. Male sparrowhawks have steely-grey backs with reddish barring underneath. Females are larger and browner than males. In flight, both show relatively long tails and rounded wings.
At close range, a piercing yellow eye is visible. **Goshawks** are very occasionally seen in the New Forest. They are similar to sparrowhawks but the size of a buzzard.

1

5

PIGS IN PANNAGE

The New Forest is probably the last place in Britain where pigs are turned out in pannage - to forage in the autumn.

Pigs have very catholic tastes and will eat almost anything, but the main source of food at this time of year is fallen acorns. The pigs find the food supply more than adequate but fewer and fewer foresters are exercising this long-held right each year.

6 Hobby *Falco subbuteo* (L. 34cm)
The hobby is a summer visitor to the New Forest, arriving in small numbers in May and leaving again in September for African wintering grounds. Its flight is dashing and aerobatic, to the extent that it is able to catch prey such as swifts, swallows and dragonflies in flight. In flight, the wings are comparatively narrow and swept-back, giving it a scythe-like silhouette. The upperparts are slate-grey, while the underparts are white with thick dark stripes. At close range, black-and-white facial markings and orange feathering on the legs can be seen.

7 Pheasant *Phasianus colchicus* (male L. 85cm)
Pheasants were introduced to Britain, including the New Forest, from Asia. They are now quite common in woodland and are sometimes seen beside forest roads. Males are bright and gaudy with orange-brown plumage; their feathers have black streaks or bars. The head is dark but with a green or purple sheen and the face bears a large, red wattle; some males have a white collar. Females have sandy brown plumage. Male pheasants make loud, explosive calls, especially in the spring. When disturbed, these birds fly rapidly on rounded wings, but they can cover only short distances.

8 Moorhen *Gallinula chloropus* (L. 33cm)
Moorhens are a common sight beside areas of water such as Beaulieu Pond and Hatchet Pond, where they are quite accustomed to man. Elsewhere in the New Forest they tend to skulk, usually beside smaller ponds and along wet ditches. Moorhens have blackish underparts and blackish-brown upperparts. When they swim, white on the undertail is revealed. The bill is red and yellow, the legs and feet are yellow with flattened toes, and there is a white streak along the flanks. Young moorhens have spiky black feathers, a red bill and a bald head. Immature birds have grey-brown plumage.

9 Lapwing *Vanellus vanellus* (L. 30cm)
Lapwings are fairly common in the New Forest throughout the year. They prefer areas of grassy heath with short vegetation and usually occur away from sites of disturbance, such as roads and paths. Lapwings are distinctive birds, the brownish upperparts having an oily, greenish-purple sheen. The underparts are white and the head has black-and-white markings and a long crest. In flight, they have a distinctive pied appearance, rounded wings and slow, flapping wingbeats. Lapwings are also known locally as 'peewits', after their distinctive flight call.

10 Snipe *Gallinago gallinago* (L. 25cm)
The most distinctive feature of the snipe is its long bill, used for probing muddy ground for worms and other invertebrates. They breed in marshy valleys bottoms in the New Forest and sometimes feed along pond and lake margins in the winter. Snipe have brownish plumage with beautiful, delicate markings of black, white and buff. This gives them excellent camouflage among waterside vegetation where they often crouch when alarmed. In the spring, they can sometimes be seen perched on fenceposts. They also perform display flights, with the tail feathers creating a bleating sound called 'drumming'.

11 Woodcock *Scolopax rusticola* (L. 36cm)
Woodcock are unusual-looking birds with long bills and large eyes placed high on the head giving a wide field of vision. The plumage provides amazing camouflage among fallen leaves on the woodland floor. Woodcock are so confident of their disguise that, when sitting on a nest, they will not fly until almost trodden on. On spring and summer nights, the male performs a display flight, called 'roding', over his territory. He flies with slow wingbeats and utters a strange mixture of grunts and squeaks. When threatened with danger, female woodcock have been known to carry their young between their legs.

12 Curlew *Numenius arquata* (L. 56cm)
In the New Forest, curlews are typically found in wet valley mires where they nest among tussocks of grass. The bubbling 'curlew' call is an evocative sound of the more remote and inaccessible parts of the region. The curlew is a distinctive bird with an immensely long, down-curved bill which is used for probing the soil for invertebrates. The plumage is brownish with dark streaking. In flight, the wings look long and rather gull-like in shape. During the winter months, most of the New Forest's curlews move to the Solent to feed.

13 Redshank *Tringa totanus* (L. 27cm)
Redshank are often found in similar habitats to curlew and snipe in the New Forest, namely boggy heaths and valley bottoms. The plumage is brown with darker barring and streaking, and the legs and the base of the bill are a distinctive red. In flight, the wings show a conspicuous white trailing edge. Redshank have earned the nickname of 'watchdog of the marshes', because at the slightest sign of danger they take to the air uttering a shrill and persistent 'chip-chip-chip'. Most of the New Forest's breeding redshank move to the Solent to feed in winter.

14 Black-headed Gull *Larus ridibundus* (L. 38cm)
Any gull seen beside a road or pond in the New Forest is likely to be a black-headed gull. Although they do not breed within the boundaries of the Forest itself, there is a huge colony at Needs Ore Point at the mouth of the Beaulieu River. Being scavenging birds, they have learnt to visit places such as picnic sites for scraps of food. During the summer months, black-headed gulls have a dark brown hood which is absent in winter. The legs and bill are reddish and, in flight, the wings show a leading white edge.

15 Woodpigeon *Columba palumbus* (L. 40cm)
As their name suggests, woodpigeons are found in woodland and forest of all kinds. At close range, the subtle pinkish-grey plumage can be seen together with the yellow bill and eye. On the neck there are dark and white patches and, in flight, conspicuous white bars on the wings can be seen. Woodpigeons build a seemingly precarious nest of twigs, arranged in the fork of a branch. The young are fed on a liquid known as 'crop milk', regurgitated by the parents. Woodpigeons are often associated with farmland and are most common around the periphery of the New Forest.

16 Cuckoo *Cuculus canorus* (L. 33cm)
The unmistakable call of the cuckoo is often the first herald of spring in the New Forest. Birdwatchers vie with each other to hear the first one each year, and a typical date would be in the third week of April. Most cuckoos have grey plumage with paler, barred underparts. Juveniles and some females, however, have brown plumage. In flight, they can look very much like a small bird of prey such as a sparrowhawk. Cuckoos lay their eggs in the nests of other birds and have no role in bringing up their young. Meadow pipits and dunnocks are typical hosts.

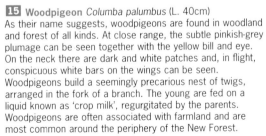

17 **Tawny Owl** *Strix aluco* (L. 38cm)
The familiar nocturnal call of the tawny owl can be heard in most areas of woodland in the New Forest, as well as in surprisingly urban sites such as the outskirts of Lyndhurst. The bird itself is more difficult to see and hides among tangled leaves during the daytime, the brown, streaked plumage affording excellent camouflage. Occasionally, however, small birds may discover the whereabouts of a roosting owl and mob it. Tawny owls feed mainly on small mammals such as mice and voles.

18 **Nightjar** *Caprimulgus europaeus* (L. 28cm)
The nightjar is perhaps the most unusual New Forest bird. It has beautifully marked plumage which provides superb camouflage against the heathland floor during the day.
At dusk, the nightjar takes to the wing, hawking for moths with its huge gape. The large eyes, kept almost shut during the daytime, give it excellent night vision. Because of their habits and camouflage, nightjars are difficult to see well. Visit an area of heathland such as Beaulieu Road Station at dusk in May or June, however, and you should hear their strange, purring, sewing-machine-like calls, often delivered for extended periods.

19 **Green Woodpecker** *Picus viridis* (L. 30cm)
Sometimes known as the 'yaffle-bird' because of its loud call, the green woodpecker is a fairly common New Forest bird. It has a liking for ants and, unlike other British woodpeckers, often feeds on the ground. Woodland rides and lawn-like areas of nibbled grass are favoured sites. As their name suggests, green woodpeckers have greenish plumage and red on the crown. One of the most noticeable features, however, is the yellow rump visible as the bird flies away from the observer. Nests are made in holes excavated in large trees and, during the breeding season, green woodpeckers become very secretive.

20 Great Spotted Woodpecker
Dendrocopus major (L. 23cm)
The great spotted is the best known of the New Forest's
woodpecker species. Its plumage is mostly black and white
but the undertail is red and males have a red nape.
Great spotted woodpeckers drum loudly, especially in the
spring, by rapping branches and tree trunks with their bill.
They also utter a loud and shrill alarm call. In flight, the wings
look very rounded and show distinct black-and-white barring.
Great spotted woodpeckers nest in holes in tree trunks.

21 Swallow *Hirundo rustica* (L. 19cm)
The swallow is a summer visitor to the region, present
from April to September. It is recognised by its blue-black
upperparts, white underparts and red face and throat. There
are long tail streamers which are longer in the male than the
female. In the New Forest, swallows are seen feeding on the
wing for insects around houses and over areas of water such
as Hatchet Pond. They often perch on wires and in the
autumn, prior to migration, they sometimes gather in large
numbers. Swallows sometimes mix with **house martins**,
small black-and-white birds with conspicuous white rumps.

22 Meadow Pipit *Anthus pratensis* (L. 14.5cm)
Drier areas of heath, especially where patches of low grass
flourish, are the preferred habitat of the meadow pipit.
At first glance it is a rather nondescript bird, the upperparts
brown with dark streaking and the underparts white with
thrush-like spotting. A closer look, however, reveals quite an
attractive bird, despite its sombre colouring. **Tree pipits** are
very similar and also occur in the New Forest, but as summer
visitors only. They prefer areas of open woodland and are
best known for their thin, repetitive song, often delivered in
flight.

23 Woodlark *Lullula arborea* (L. 15cm)
The woodlark makes up for its uniform, sandy-brown plumage with its song, one of the most beautiful of all British birds. Sometimes delivered in flight, it is often rendered as 'tu-de-lu-de-lu' and can be heard at almost any time of day from April to June. A close look at a woodlark reveals its rather short-tailed appearance. The upperparts are brown with dark streaking and a pale line above the eye separates the orange-brown cheeks from the dark crown. In the New Forest, woodlarks are often found on recently burnt areas where the ground is still charred.

24 Pied Wagtail *Motacilla alba yarrellii* (L. 18.5cm)
Pied wagtails are familiar New Forest birds found around car parks and beside ponds and lakes. Their name is extremely descriptive, since their appearance is distinctly pied black and white, and they continually wag their tails. Young birds and winter adults show much less black and are generally paler than summer adults. The pied wagtail has a distinctive 'chissick' call, often given in flight which is low and undulating. On the ground they typically run fast, chasing after insects which they sometimes pursue in flight.

25 Jay *Garrulus glandarius* (L. 35cm)
Jays are most frequently seen as they fly up from a wooded roadside verge or along a forest ride, revealing a striking white rump. They spend a lot of time foraging on the ground and, in the autumn, search vigilantly for acorns. Jays are rather unusual members of the crow family and have pinkish plumage and dark wings bearing a blue, black and white chequered patch. They are noisy birds and their raucous screeches are a familiar sound in most wooded parts of the Forest. Generally speaking, they are rather wary of man.

26 Jackdaw *Corvus monedula* (L. 33cm)
These bold scavengers can be seen around picnic sites and heathland car parks in the Forest. The plumage is mostly dark but the neck is rather grey. One of the most striking features is the pale iris. On the ground, jackdaws have a curious, shuffling gait while the flight is fast with rapid wingbeats. They nest in holes in old trees and sometimes in houses or outbuildings. In the winter, jackdaws sometimes gather in large flocks and mix with other members of the crow family. Typical calls include a sharp 'chack' and a slurred 'kee-arr'.

27 Wren *Troglodytes troglodytes* (L. 10cm)
The wren is one of the smallest birds likely to be seen in the New Forest. It is also one of the commonest although, in severe winters, its numbers plummet. Wrens are insect-feeders and creep around rather secretively among the undergrowth. The best indication of their presence is often a loud rattling or churring call, or their surprisingly loud and musical song. Wrens have mainly brown plumage and a rather dumpy appearance, the short tail often held cocked vertically. They can be found in almost any habitat in the Forest.

INCLOSURES

The need to maintain the regenerative cycle of tree growth and ensure a supply of timber in the New Forest has been recognised throughout much of its long history.

Since the 17th century, a variety of fenced inclosures have been created, some subsequently being enshrined in law. The purpose of these inclosures was to keep deer and stock animals out and prevent damage caused by grazing and browsing. Some inclosures surrounded old coppices with mature standard trees while others were planted with oaks. Sadly, the network of inclosures has been rather neglected in recent years. Not surprisingly, inclosures in which grazing animals have invaded show few signs of regeneration.

The height to which animals can eat foliage is called a 'browse line' — seen here on this holly tree.

28 Blackcap *Sylvia atricapilla* (L. 14cm)

Blackcaps are summer visitors, arriving in May and leaving again in August. The male is aptly named because it does indeed have a black cap; the cheeks are greyish, the underparts pale and the upperparts brown. Females resemble males except that the cap is chestnut rather than black. Typical blackcap habitats include dense understorey vegetation in woodland and mature gardens; the birds feed on insects. Males have a rich and melodic song, usually sung from within the cover of a bush. Occasionally, small numbers of blackcaps may overwinter if the weather is mild.

29 Dartford Warbler *Sylvia undata* (L. 13cm)

If any bird could be said to be the symbol of the New Forest, then it is the Dartford warbler. The heathlands in this part of Hampshire are its stronghold and it is a year-round resident in areas of tall gorse. Dartford warblers are rather difficult to see well although they occasionally perch in an exposed position to view intruders into their territory. IThey have blue-grey upperparts and reddish underparts. The tail is rather long and sometimes cocked slightly. When alarmed, Dartford warblers utter a buzzing churr. They are completely protected by the law and must not be disturbed in any way.

30 Willow Warbler

Phylloscopus trochilus (L. 11.5cm)

This tiny warbler is a summer visitor to Britain, arriving in April and leaving again in September. In appearance, it is rather drab, with greyish-brown upperparts and paler underparts. As such, it is very similar to the **chiffchaff**, another summer visitor to the region. Fortunately, however, the willow warbler does have a distinctive song, comprising a tuneful series of descending notes. That of the chiffchaff, on the other hand, is a rapid series of 'chiff-chaff, chiff-chaff' notes. Willow warblers are found in patches of willow and birch, and search actively among the leaves for insects.

31 Goldcrest *Regulus regulus* (L. 9cm)

The goldcrest is the smallest bird of the region. It feeds actively among branches and foliage, searching for insects and uttering its thin, high-pitched call. Goldcrests have rather sombre, grey-brown plumage, enlivened by striking white wingbars and a bold, yellow crown, bordered with black. In the New Forest, they are usually associated with areas of mature conifers although, in winter, they can occur in almost any type of woodland. At this time of year, they are sometimes seen in mixed feeding flocks of small birds, such as tits and nuthatches.

32 Spotted Flycatcher *Muscicapa striata* (L. 14cm)

A summer visitor to Europe, the spotted flycatcher arrives in the New Forest in May and leaves again in September. Its plumage is rather nondescript, having brown upperparts and pale underparts with faint streaking on the breast. The bird can be recognised, however, by its habits.

Spotted flycatchers habitually perch on exposed branches overlooking a clearing or mature garden. From here, they embark on short sorties after flying insects, usually returning to the same perch. Typical habitats would include woodland clearings, often near water, and mature gardens.

33 Stonechat *Saxicola torquata* (L. 12cm)

The stonechat is a delightful resident of the New Forest's heathlands. It is often seen perched high on a spray of gorse or on a post, cursing intruders into its territory with a loud 'tchack' alarm call, rather like the sound of two pebbles being knocked together. The male is resplendent with a black head, brown back, orange breast and white on the neck. The female is browner with more subdued colours than the male. In the New Forest, stonechats can be found on almost any area of heath but are usually associated with patches of tall, straggly gorse.

28

29

31

32

36 Blackbird *Turdus merula* (L. 24cm)
The blackbird needs very little introduction and is quite common and widespread in the New Forest, being found in woodlands and clearings. Males are distinctive with their all-black plumage and yellow bill and eye-ring. Females, on the other hand, are a rather uniform brown. Blackbirds typically feed on the ground, searching for earthworms and other invertebrates, and often favour the pony-nibbled areas of grass so typical of the New Forest. In the spring, the male sings a tuneful and attractive song, delivered mainly at dawn and dusk.

37 Song Thrush *Turdus philomelos* (L. 22cm)
A powerful, tuneful song, the phrases of which are often repeated two or three times, announces the presence of the song thrush. Favouring areas of mature, open woodland and gardens, the bird is fairly common in the New Forest. Like its relative, the blackbird, the song thrush feeds mainly on the ground, often standing rigid for quite long periods, staring at the ground for movement in search of worms. It is a year-round resident in the Forest, nesting in the fork of a tree. Unlike some other species of thrush, it is seldom gregarious in the winter months.

34 Redstart *Phoenicurus phoenicurus* (L. 14cm)
From May to August, redstarts can be found in areas of deciduous woodland in the New Forest. They particularly like open woodland with trees mature enough to provide holes for nesting in. The male is an attractive bird showing a black head and throat with white and grey on the forecrown, a dark back, and orange-red underparts and tail. The female is more uniformly brown, but still shows the striking orange-red tail. In both sexes, the tail is constantly quivered. From dawn onwards, the melancholy and musical song can be heard, often delivered from the same perch used for fly-catching sallies.

35 Robin *Erithacus rubecula* (L. 14cm)
The robin is a year-round resident in the New Forest and occurs in a wide variety of habitats from woodland to mature gardens. In some areas, such as woodland car parks, they have become quite tame. Adult robins are unmistakable, with a bright orange-red face and breast. Young birds, however, are more uniform brown and covered in pale spots. Robins can be heard singing at almost any time of year although the musical, rippling tones are more muted during the winter months. They also utter a sharp 'tic-tic' when alarmed.

38 Blue Tit *Parus caeruleus* (L. 12cm)
Blue tits are common in deciduous woodlands and gardens throughout the New Forest. They are attractive birds with yellow underparts, a bluish-grey cap and black-and-white on the face with a black line through the eye. In the winter months they can sometimes be seen in small flocks, often mixing with other species such as great tits and siskins. Blue tits are quite vocal birds, uttering a variety of harsh, chattering calls. The song comprises two reedy notes followed by a trill. Blue tits nest in holes in trees and readily take to nest boxes provided by thoughtful foresters.

39 Great Tit *Parus major* (L. 14cm)
The great tit is distinguished by its greenish upperparts and black head, which has white cheeks. The yellow underparts are divided down the middle by a thick, black line, continuous with the black throat. Great tits often mix with blue tits in the winter and can be told by size alone. Like their close relatives, they also nest in holes in trees and readily take to nest boxes. Great tits feed mainly on insects, especially in summer. In winter, however, they will visit bird feeders for peanuts. The loud song is sometimes rendered 'tea-cher, tea-cher, tea-cher'.

45

41 Treecreeper *Certhia familiaris* (L. 13cm)
Areas of mature deciduous and coniferous woodland, such as along the Ornamental Drive at Rhinefield, are the favoured habitats of the treecreeper. Its name is indeed apt, since it creeps up the trunks of trees, extracting insects from the bark with its curved, tweezer-like bill. The treecreeper's plumage is streaked brown on the upperparts and white on the underparts. They feed characteristically by working their way around and up a tree trunk in a spiral fashion; they then fly down to the base of an adjacent tree and repeat the process.

42 Chaffinch *Fringilla coelebs* (L. 15cm)
The chaffinch is rather common in the New Forest and can be seen around most woodland car parks. They often feed on the ground, searching for seeds and nuts, and can frequently be seen in small flocks during the winter months. The male chaffinch is an attractive bird with pinkish underparts, a bluish nape and crown, a reddish-brown back and a pale green rump. The female is a more uniform brown, and both sexes have two white wingbars, most conspicuous in flight. The song of the chaffinch is a descending, tuneful rattle, ending in a flourish; the call is a loud 'pink'.

43 Greenfinch *Carduelis chloris* (L. 14.5cm)
Bright flashes of yellow on the wings and sides of the tail are good identification features of the greenfinch when seen in flight. The male has subtle greenish-olive plumage which is paler below than above. The female, on the other hand, has more muted coloration and is streaked brownish-buff. Even when at rest, both sexes show a conspicuous yellow bar along the length of the wing. Greenfinches feed mainly on seeds and will sometimes visit bird feeders. The variable song often includes a distinctive wheezing note.

44 Siskin *Carduelis spinus* (L. 12cm)
At first glance, a siskin resembles a miniature greenfinch. However, the small size soon becomes apparent, as do the two yellow wingbars seen in both sexes. The male has well marked, mostly yellowish-green plumage: the cap and bib are black, the wingbars are defined by black and there is dark streaking on the back and flanks. The female is a more uniform brown with darker streaking. Siskins are more usually seen in the New Forest during the winter. They gather in large flocks, sometimes mixed with redpolls, and feed in alders and birches near the tops of the trees.

40 Nuthatch *Sitta europaea* (L. 14cm)
Superficially resembling a small, dumpy woodpecker in appearance, the nuthatch is the only British bird that habitually climbs head-first down tree trunks. It has blue-grey upperparts and orange-buff underparts except for a white throat. The stout claws and toes give a good grip on bark and the chisel-like bill is used to extract insect grubs. Nuthatches nest in holes in tree trunks, plastering the entrances with mud to create the right-sized hole. They are common in the New Forest and mostly associated with areas of mature, deciduous woodland.

45 Goldfinch *Carduelis carduelis* (L. 14cm)
For all its small size, the goldfinch is one of Britain's most colourful birds. The head is a bold mixture of red, white and black, the back is buffish and the black wings show broad yellow wingbars. These latter features, together with the white rump, are best seen in flight which is always accompanied by delightful, tinkling calls. The sight and sound of a flock of goldfinches (known as a 'charm') is a memorable one. In the New Forest, goldfinches are attracted to areas of waste ground and disturbed soil where seed-rich plants such as thistles thrive.

46 Linnet *Carduelis cannabina* (L. 13cm)
Linnets can be found in the New Forest throughout the year. During spring and summer, pairs favour patches of rank gorse on the heathlands where they breed, while in winter, small flocks roam far and wide. The male linnet is underrated by many birdwatchers. In spring, the head and underparts are grey-buff, the forecrown and breast band are red, and the back is chestnut. In flight, the pale rump and sides to the tail are striking. The female linnet is rather nondescript, having uniform brown plumage. The male's song is a mixture of tinkling and twittering sounds.

47 Crossbill *Loxia curvirostra* (L. 16cm)
The crossbill gets its name from its extraordinary bill, the tips of which overlap and are used to extract seeds from conifer cones. Crossbills are quite colourful birds, males being deep red and females yellowish-green. They nest early in the year — sometimes starting as early as February. By May, roaming family groups can sometimes be seen in isolated clumps of conifers in the New Forest. The best time to see them, however, is in early winter by walking through a mature spruce plantation and listening for the sharp 'chuk' calls and the sound of falling pine cones.

48 Reed Bunting *Emberiza schoeniclus* (L. 15.5cm)
In the New Forest, reed buntings are widespread but never especially numerous. Clumps of birches and willows, growing beside streams or in boggy valleys, are favoured areas but they are by no means restricted to this habitat. The male is a distinctive bird in spring, with a black head and throat, and a white moustachial stripe continuous with the white nape and underparts; the upperparts are brownish and streaked. In winter, the male loses the distinct head markings and is rather similar to the female with brown, heavily streaked plumage.

49 Yellowhammer *Emberiza citrinella* (L. 16.5cm)
The male yellowhammer is a colourful bird with mainly yellow underparts and chestnut-brown upperparts. The head is mainly yellow with black markings on the crown and through the eye. The female is more uniform buff-brown but the underparts, in particular, still have a yellowish wash. Yellowhammers are found in areas of dry scrub in the New Forest, especially among bushes of blackthorn or hawthorn. In the spring, the male announces himself with a distinctive song, often rendered 'a little bit of bread but no cheese'. In winter, yellowhammers may be found in small flocks.

46

48

49

MARL PITS

Here and there in the New Forest, keen-eyed visitors can find collections of marl pits long-since abandoned and now teeming with pond life.

Marl, a type of chalk-rich clay, was dug in the past for two important purposes. Firstly, it was used in the construction of cob-walled houses and secondly it was used to improve the gravelly, acid soils on nearby agricultural land. A good number of rather overgrown marl pits can be found at Crockford Bridge.

Autumn Lady's tresses is a typical flower of chalk-rich clay.

MAMMALS

50 Roe Deer *Capreolus capreolus* (H. 70cm)
The roe deer is the smallest species of deer likely to be encountered in the New Forest. It is often a solitary animal but may occasionally be seen in single sex groups of two to four animals. For much of the year, roe deer feed on the leaves of bramble and so are usually found in areas where this rambling plant grows in profusion, such as woodland rides and scrub patches. If spotted by an observer, they will sometimes 'freeze', staring back at the intruder and showing their large ears and distinctively marked muzzle. If alarmed, they quickly disappear into the undergrowth, revealing a white rump as they go.

51 Fallow Deer *Dama dama* (H. 85cm)
Fallow deer are thought to have been reintroduced to Britain by the Normans, having died out during the last Ice Age; records from the New Forest date back to medieval times. Until comparatively recently they were still hunted, this being the original reason for their introduction. Fallow deer are herd animals and small groups can be seen in many parts of the forest. The best place to observe them, however, is at the Bolderwood deer inclosure where they are accustomed to man. Visit in October and you may witness the annual rut where males battle with each other for the right to mate.

52 Red Deer *Cervus elaphus* (H. 120cm)
The red deer can also trace its documented ancestry back to medieval times, having been important for its venison and the 'sport' it provided. It is our largest species of deer and the New Forest population comprises several hundred animals. The best areas to look for them are around Burley and Brockenhurst although, despite their size, they can be surprisingly difficult to locate. Males do battle during the autumn rutting season for the right to mate: loud bellowing and the sound of clashing antlers carry for a considerable distance on still mornings in October.

53 Fox *Vulpes vulpes* (L. 100cm)
The way most people see a fox in the New Forest is in car headlights while driving at night or as a road casualty.

Because persecution still persists in all its forms, they are understandably retiring during the hours of daylight. Having said this, however, plenty of visitors still see foxes in broad daylight: cubs playing in the spring sunshine outside an earth or a full-grown fox running across a heath are both memorable sights. Foxes feed on a wide range of animals, from small mammals to insects.

54 Badger *Meles meles* (L. 85cm)
With its black-and-white striped face and low, shuffling gait, badgers are easy to recognise. They are, however, rather difficult to see, being strictly nocturnal animals which spend the day in underground setts. Young animals sometimes play above ground during the day but badgers are mostly seen crossing roads at night. A few of the New Forest's setts are regularly watched and the animals are consequently accustomed to man. Most setts, however, are not used to the smell of humans and should not be disturbed in any way. At one time, badgers were persecuted but now, thankfully, they are fully protected by the law.

55 Grey Squirrel *Sciurus carolinensis* (L. 100cm)
The grey squirrel was introduced into Britain and is not an altogether welcome addition to our native fauna. Whatever its shortcomings, however, it is probably here to stay and is easy to see in the New Forest. Some are bold enough to visit car parks for scraps of food, but most keep to the trees in the areas of deciduous and mixed woodland that they favour. Grey squirrels build large twig nests, called dreys, high in the branches. It is here that they give birth to their young and shelter at night. Grey squirrels are active throughout the year, feeding primarily on nuts and fruits.

56 Wood Mouse *Apodemus sylvaticus* (L. 14cm)
Despite its name, the wood mouse occurs in a wide range of habitats including gardens, hedgerows and heaths, as well as woodland. Most active at night, it spends the day in underground burrows where food is cached and the young are reared. At night, they come out to forage on the ground and sometimes among the undergrowth. It is then that they fall victim to predators such as tawny owls and foxes. Wood mouse numbers are highly dependent on the availability of food: when there is a good supply of nuts, seeds and berries in autumn, they flourish; in bad years, their numbers plummet.

57 Yellow-necked Mouse *Apodemus flavicollis* (L.17cm)
The yellow-necked mouse is a true woodland species. It is larger and heavier than its relative, the wood mouse, and has bigger ears and a relatively longer tail. Its most distinctive feature, however, is the yellow-buff band across its chest, not always easy to see as the mouse scurries across the forest floor. If you sit patiently in an area of mature, deciduous woodland, you might be lucky enough to see one foraging in the late afternoon. Yellow-necked mice sometimes move into houses, churches and outbuildings at the onset of winter weather.

58 Harvest Mouse *Micromys minutus* (L. 8cm)
The harvest mouse is the smallest species of mouse in Britain and weighs only a few grams when full grown. The mouse itself is seen less frequently than its nest, which is a beautifully constructed ball of woven grass stems, built among grass stems, meadow plants or sometimes in bramble clumps. They can use their tails to grip grass stems as they clamber among the vegetation. Inside the spherical nest, a family of four or five young are raised, and harvest mice also build winter nests as well. Not surprisingly, they suffer heavy mortality from predators such as weasels or kestrels.

59 Short-tailed Vole *Microtus agrestis* (L. 11cm)
Together with populations of other small mammals, the numbers of short-tailed voles help sustain the populations of the New Forest's predators. Weasels, foxes, kestrels and tawny owls take a heavy toll and, during the winter months, visiting hen harriers and short-eared owls also feed on them. Short-tailed voles have rather compact bodies and, as their name suggests, somewhat stumpy tails. They spend most of the time in burrows just below the surface of the soil. Almost any grassy area in or around the New Forest is likely to have numbers of short-tailed voles in residence.

REPTILES

60 Common Lizard *Lacerta vivipara* (L. 14cm)
Being cold-blooded animals, common lizards love to bask in the sunshine. Walk across an area of New Forest heathland on a warm spring day and you will be unlucky not to see a few adorning areas of bare soil and scurrying for cover at your approach. Common lizards hibernate during the winter months but emerge by about March or April and begin feeding on insects. The female gives birth to live young, the eggs having hatched internally. The young are dark at first, and many fall victim to heathland predators, including adders and kestrels.

61 Sand Lizard *Lacerta agilis* (L. 15cm)
Sand lizards are much scarcer than their relative, the common lizard. In the New Forest, they are restricted to a few areas of heathland, mainly in the west of the region, their stronghold in Britain being on the Dorset heathlands. They are larger and bulkier than their relatives. In the spring, males acquire a bright green coloration which is used in breeding displays. Sand lizards feed mainly on insects and spiders. Like most other reptiles, they sunbathe to warm their bodies, especially in the spring; this is the best time of year to observe them. During the summer months temperatures are too hot and they are much more difficult to see.

62 Adder *Vipera berus* (L. 35cm)
Although their background colour may vary, the zig-zag markings along the back of the adder make it a distinctive and unmistakable animal. They are Britain's only poisonous snake, the venom being used to kill small prey such as lizards, voles or young birds. A healthy adult human is unlikely to suffer any lasting effects: the shock of being bitten is usually more stressful than the venom itself. Adders often sunbathe on paths or sometimes on clumps of heather. They are an integral part of the ecology of New Forest heathlands and should be treated with respect as well as caution.

63 Smooth Snake *Coronella austriaca* (L. 50cm)
The smooth snake is an extremely rare animal in Britain, the New Forest being one of the few remaining habitats where it still occurs. As with other reptiles, the best chances of observation come in spring when the snakes frequently sunbathe to increase their body temperature. Like that other rare reptile, the sand lizard, smooth snakes are completely protected by the law and must not be disturbed in any way. In other parts of southern England where they occur, smooth snakes are threatened by habitat loss. In the New Forest, however, the main threat comes from heathland fires.

68

64

BUTTERFLIES

64 **Brimstone** *Gonepteryx rhamni*
The brimstone is often the first butterfly to be seen in the spring. On warm days, from late March onwards, bright yellow males and pale yellow females can be seen flying along woodland rides and visiting willow catkins to feed. The reason for this butterfly's early appearance is that it hibernates, often in clumps of ivy. Butterflies appear again in mid-summer, the new brood having grown from eggs laid in the spring on alder buckthorn. Both the caterpillar and the pupa are very well camouflaged among the leaves of this plant.

65 **Speckled Wood** *Pararge aegeria*
The speckled wood is a fairly common woodland butterfly and typically occurs in sunny woodland glades and rides which are not overgrazed. It is a real sun-lover and, even in rather gloomy settings, will settle on a leaf caught in a shaft of sunlight. Another interesting aspect of this butterfly's life is that the males are rather territorial and they engage in mid-air battles over the right to a particular patch of sunny ride. Several broods appear from spring to autumn, with a considerable amount of overlap. This effectively means that speckled woods can be seen from April until late September. The caterpillars eat grass.

66 **Ringlet** *Aphantopus hyperantus*
Grassy woodland rides and meadows are favourite haunts of the ringlet, whose caterpillars feed on the leaves of grasses. The butterfly has rather dark, smoky brown upperwings which are somewhat difficult to observe well since it is constantly active and seldom rests with the wings spread. When resting on dull days, or feeding on the flowers of bramble, the underwing is usually easier to observe. It is a rich brown with black eyespots, highlighted with white. Ringlets are seen on the wing during June and July and have a rather fluttering flight.

67 **Meadow Brown** *Maniola jurtina*
The meadow brown is one of the commonest butterflies in southern England. In the New Forest, it is to be found wherever there are grassy areas, the leaves providing food for the caterpillars. Meadow browns are on the wing from June to September. They are fond of visiting flowers such as thistles, knapweeds and brambles and sometimes cluster together in sizeable groups on particularly good sources of nectar. Males and females can be distinguished by their upperwings: males are a uniform dark brown with an eyespot on the forewing; females have a broad orange-buff band on the forewings.

68 Grayling *Hipparchia semele*
Graylings can be found wherever there are bare patches of soil or gravel on the heathlands of the New Forest. They can be rather difficult to locate until they fly because, when resting on the ground, they orientate their closed wings so that no shadow is cast. The underwings are often held so that the eyespots on the forewing are not visible and the patterning on the hindwing affords excellent camouflage. The butterflies are seen on the wing during June and July and are best looked for along bare heathland paths. The caterpillars feed on grass.

HEATHLAND FIRES

Fire has long been used in the management of heathlands in the New Forest and its legitimate use is permitted by law.

The effects of fire are to control invasion by trees such as birch and Scots pine and to promote the fresh growth of grasses and heathers. When employed sensibly, the overall effect can be beneficial for wildlife. For example, woodlarks thrive on newly burnt areas and fire can contain the growth of gorse at an optimum level for breeding Dartford warblers. Uncontrolled fires, which have become all too frequent during recent summers, are a disaster, however, threatening the lives of people as well as destroying countless plants and animals.

69 White Admiral *Limenitis camilla*
The white admiral is one of the speciality insects of the New Forest, although it is much rarer than it used to be. It flies during July and August. The adult butterfly is extremely fond of bramble blossom but is quick to take flight if disturbed. The flight is rapid and powerful, often with long glides.
White admirals are distinctively marked. The upperwings are smoky black with a broad band of white running through the wings. The underwings are orange-brown, with numerous white and dark markings. The adult insect is seldom found far from clumps of woodland honeysuckle, the foodplant of the caterpillar.

70 Silver-washed Fritillary
Argynnis paphia
To the butterfly enthusiast, there are few sights more evocative of a summer's day than the sight of a silver-washed fritillary flying along a sunny New Forest glade. On the wing in July and August, these butterflies delight in visiting bramble blossoms in search of nectar.
The upperwing of the silver-washed fritillary is a rich orange-brown with dark spots. In contrast, the underwing, and that of the hindwing in particular, is greenish with a silver sheen. The caterpillars feed on the leaves of violets and are covered in spiky hairs.

71 Marsh Fritillary *Eurodryas aurinia*
The marsh fritillary is a rather enigmatic butterfly: it regularly has disastrous years after which it would be supposed that it had been wiped out. But reappear it does on the boggy heaths where devil's-bit scabious, the foodplant of its hairy, black caterpillar, grows. Marsh fritillaries generally appear in

late May and early June but even in good years they can be difficult to see. This is because they are sun-loving insects; the moment the sun disappears, they tumble into the vegetation and are seemingly impossible to locate.

72 Purple Hairstreak *Quercusia quercus*
In all the stages of its life-cycle, the purple hairstreak is seldom found far from oak trees. The eggs are laid on the buds, the caterpillars eat the leaves and the pupae are attached to the twigs. Colonies of butterflies can be seen flying around the tops of the trees during July and early August. They are very active and seldom descend to ground level on sunny days. On dull days or after rain, however, they can sometimes be seen sitting on leaves in the undergrowth beneath oaks. Purple hairstreaks have grey underwings and dark upperwings with a purple sheen.

73 Green Hairstreak *Callophrys rubi*
The green hairstreak is a characteristic heathland butterfly in the New Forest. One of the favourite foodplants of the caterpillar is gorse, and during May and June adult butterflies can be seen flying actively around clumps of this spiky plant. Green hairstreaks can be surprisingly difficult to see, even on a sunny day. In flight, they can be almost impossible to follow, the slightly reflective scales on the underwing making them seem invisible against a bright sky. When resting on vegetation, the green underwings afford superb camouflage.

74 Silver-studded Blue *Plebejus argus*
During the months of July and August, the silver-studded blue is, without doubt, the most typical butterfly of the New Forest heaths. On sunny mornings, small groups can be seen flying actively around clumps of ling and occasionally pausing to settle and sunbathe, often resting upside down. Silver-studded blues have underwings beautifully marked with grey, orange, black and white. The upperwing is blue in the male and brown with a fringe of orange spots in the female. Almost any expanse of New Forest heath is likely to have silver-studded blues, although Beaulieu Road Station is particularly good.

76 **Broad-bodied Chaser**
Libellula depressa
One of the New Forest's most attractive dragonflies is the broad-bodied chaser. It has unmarked wings and, as the name suggests, a broad, flattened body. In males, the body is pale blue, while in females it is orange-brown with dark spots. Broad-bodied chasers often disperse a long distance from water after they have emerged and can be seen flying over wide open heaths. After a few weeks, however, they return to the pond to mate. Males, in particular, take up territories which they defend against other males. The nymph is flattened and hairy; it lives in mud and debris on the pond bottom.

77 **Southern Hawker**
Aeshna cyanea
The southern hawker is a summer-flying species of dragonfly, being seen on the wing from July to September. Keen-eyed observers can sometimes see adults emerging from their nymphal skins, resting on emergent pond vegetation. This process of metamorphosis usually starts around dawn but continues for a few hours until the dragonfly's wings are strong enough for flight. Southern hawkers have attractively marked bodies with markings of lime green and blue. They are extremely active insects and can catch quite sizeable insects in flight.

75 **Four-spot Chaser**
Libellula quadrimaculata
The four-spot chaser is an extremely active dragonfly. It can sometimes be seen resting to catch the sun on sprays of ling or on pondside vegetation. As soon as it spots an intruder with its large eyes, however, it is off with a clatter of whirring wings. Four-spot chasers spend almost all of their year-long lives as nymphal stages living in ponds in the New Forest. In June, the adults emerge and disperse from the pond for a few weeks before returning to mate and lay eggs. The best identification features are the four dark spots, one on each of the wings.

78

78 Golden-ringed Dragonfly
Cordulegaster boltonii
This is one of the largest species of dragonfly in
Britain and is reasonably common in the New
Forest. The nymphs take two or more years to
develop and live among the gravel and mud on
the bottom of slow-flowing streams and ditches.
The adults, which have beautiful black and yellow
markings on their bodies, range far and wide over
the heathland. They are perhaps easiest to see
well on dull days, when they lose all energy and
rest motionless among the vegetation. Golden-
ringed dragonflies can be seen flying during July
and August.

79 Common Darter *Sympetrum striolatum*
As its name suggests, the common darter is
perhaps the most numerous dragonfly in the New
Forest. It appears relatively late in the season,
often not until August, and continues flying until
the first severe frosts of autumn, sometimes until
early November. When newly emerged, common
darters are dull orange-tan but they gradually
acquire a deep red coloration to their bodies.
The nymphs live in almost any type of waterbody
in the New Forest, ranging from tiny heathland
pools and ditches to large ponds and lakes.
They take a year to reach maturity.

77

79

81

82

83

80 **Common Blue Damselfly** *Enallagma cyathigerum*
There are several species of blue damselfly found in the New Forest but, as its name suggests, this is the most common and widespread of them. The body colour is sky blue and there are black markings on the segments of the abdomen. Like all damselflies, the common blue holds its wings over the abdomen at rest and has eyes which are widely spaced apart. These features readily distinguish them from dragonflies which hold the wings out flat at rest and have eyes which touch in most species. The nymphal stages of the common blue damselfly live in heathland pools and the adults do not stray far.

81 **Southern Blue Damselfly** *Coenagrion mercuriale*
The New Forest is the last stronghold of the southern blue damselfly. It lives in very boggy places such as pools beside heathland mires and streams in valley bottoms, typically where bog myrtle grows in profusion. On dull days in late May and early June, one of the best ways of seeing this scarce insect is to look for it resting on sprays of this aromatic plant. Superficially, the southern blue damselfly resembles several other species of blue damselfly found in southern England. However, a close inspection of the upper surface of the abdomen, near the base of the wings, reveals a marking similar to the Greek sign of Mercury.

82 **Small Red Damselfly** *Ceriagrion tenellum*
The small red damselfly is a rather scarce species in Britain which has its stronghold in the New Forest. Its nymphal stages live in ponds, varying in size from small but permanent heathland pools to water bodies the size of Hatchet Pond. Because it is a weak flier, the small red damselfly is usually found around the water's edge and pairs can sometimes be seen egg-laying at the surface in June. It could possibly be confused with the large red damselfly, but at a length of 40mm, as opposed to 30mm, this is a noticeably bulkier insect with brighter colours.

83 **The Demoiselle** *Calopteryx virgo*
In June and July, these attractive insects can be seen fluttering along New Forest streams, sizeable groups sometimes gathering together in certain spots. The male can be recognised by its bluish wings and the metallic sheen, not only to the wings but to the body as well. In females, the colour is brownish, but they still show a bluish sheen. The banded agrion (*Calopteryx splendens*) is similar, but the male has clear wings with a large, bluish blotch. The nymphs of the demoiselle live in the silt on the stream bed.

THE SOLENT

The southern border of the New Forest stretches almost as far as the Solent, the stretch of water lying between mainland Hampshire and the Isle of Wight.

While on a visit to the New Forest, a few hours spent on the coast can provide an interesting alternative to woodland and heath habitats. Any accessible point between Calshot Spit and Lymington is likely to be good. Waders and wildfowl are at their best during the winter months while saltmarsh flowers at Hurst Spit are best in August and September.

84 **Large Marsh Grasshopper** *Stethophyma grossum*
The large marsh grasshopper is the largest species in Britain
— 40mm in length — with its stronghold in the New Forest.
It has a rather restricted habitat preference, being found only
on floating bogs where a carpet of green sphagnum moss
indicates a terrain treacherous to the foot. The insect is
beautifully marked with yellow, black and red, and males are
smaller than females. If disturbed, large marsh grasshoppers
are capable of flying comparatively long distances, taking
them out of reach of potential predators. They are best
looked for, with due care, in July and August.

85 **Mottled Grasshopper** *Myrmeleotettix maculatus*
Dry areas of heathland are the favoured habitat of the mottled
grasshopper. On sunny days in July and August it delights in
basking on bare patches of sandy soil and is consequently
highly active if disturbed. The mottled grasshopper has a
rather variable background colour including brown, grey or
green. However, it always has bold black markings on the
body and wings and characteristically shaped antennae with
bulbous tips. In bright sunlight, the mosaic of markings
affords the mottled grasshopper excellent camouflage on
the heathland soil.

86 Bog Bush Cricket *Metrioptera brachyptera*
In common with all members of this group, the bog bush cricket has very long hind legs and antennae much longer than the body. The female has a long, curved ovipositor, resembling a dagger, used for laying eggs in plant stems. Bog bush crickets live on damp heathland in the New Forest and can be seen hopping and clambering through clumps of bell heather and cross-leaved heath during July and August. They have variable amounts of green or brown on the body which gives them good camouflage when they are motionless among the vegetation. Bog bush crickets feed on small insects.

87 Oak Bush Cricket *Meconema thalassinium*
As its name suggests, the oak bush cricket is invariably found in the vicinity of oak trees. It lives among the leaves and feeds on aphids and other small insects. The oak bush cricket has a rather translucent, pale green body with very long hind legs and antennae. The female has a long, straight ovipositor; despite its weapon-like appearance, this is harmless and used only for laying eggs. The oak bush cricket is seen mainly during August and September. It is occasionally found near ground level after rain storms and is sometimes attracted by house lights in the autumn.

88 Wood Cricket *Nemobius sylvestris*
Walk through a forested area of the New Forest with piles of fallen leaves, and you may be lucky enough to hear the strange purring chirps of the wood cricket. These engaging little insects live in loose colonies among the leaves and are best looked for in early spring or late summer. When first approached, they are rather shy and can be difficult to see well; sit and wait, however, and they will soon come scurrying out. Wood crickets have flattened bodies and long antennae. Compared to bush crickets, however, they have relatively short hind legs and can manage only short hops.

OTHER INSECTS

89 Wood Ant *Formica rufa*

The wood ant is the largest ant in the New Forest and makes huge, conspicuous nests on the forest floor. On the outside, these comprise a mound of vegetation such as twigs and pine needles and are often covered with a seething throng of ants. Watch closely and you may see some of the workers returning to the nest with caterpillars, beetles or other small invertebrates — food for the young grubs that live underground. Not surprisingly, wood ants are friends of the forester since they kill so many potentially damaging pest insects.

90 Scorpionfly *Panorpa communis*

The scorpionfly gets its name from the male's swollen tip to the abdomen, which is held arched like a scorpion's sting. Not surprisingly, at first glance, the scorpionfly looks extremely menacing: the tail end looks poised to sting and the head bears formidable mouthparts. In fact, it is a rather innocuous insect from our point of view and certainly will not sting or bite. The swollen abdomen tip contains the reproductive organs and the mouth is used for feeding on insects trapped in spiders' webs. Scorpionflies are seen from May to July and are often found in bramble clumps.

91 Stag Beetle *Lucanus cervus*

There can be few more awesome sights in the insect world than that of two male stag beetles fighting for the right to mate with a female. In fact, the antler-like projections on the head have evolved for just this purpose and are absent in the female. Stag beetles appear in warm weather in June and July. They are a woodland species, their larvae having spent the previous year burrowing through the rotting wood of a tree stump. Adult stag beetles are among the largest of British insects and are particularly impressive when in flight.

92 Green Tiger Beetle *Cicindela campestris*

Walk along almost any stretch of heathland path in May or June and you will see active, green beetles scurrying along |or taking to the wing at your approach. These are likely to be green tiger beetles which are so characteristic of this habitat in the spring. The name derives from the metallic green colour of the body and the fact that they are ferocious predators. Almost anything small enough to be tackled is considered potential prey and green tiger beetles have fearsome mouthparts which are used to dispatch caterpillars and flies.

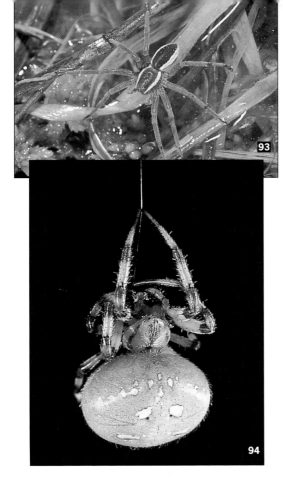

OTHER INVERTEBRATES

93 Raft Spider *Dolomedes fimbriatus*
The raft spider is the largest spider to be found in the New Forest and can hardly be confused with any other. A full-grown specimen would almost cover the palm of your hand and is attractively marked in rich brown with buff stripes on the flanks. Raft spiders live exclusively on heathland pools. Their coating of silky hairs enables them to walk on water although, if alarmed, they can dive beneath the surface with ease. Raft spiders feed on insects, such as damselflies, that become trapped on the surface of the water. They can also catch fish underwater.

94 Common Cross Spider *Araneus quadratus*
There are numerous species of spider found in the New Forest but the common cross spider is one of the most distinctive. When full grown, males are considerably smaller than females but both share a distinctive cross marking on the body. The best time of year to see them, as well as most other spiders, is in the autumn when large tracts of heathland are covered in their silky webs. The spiders feed on heathland insects trapped in the webs. At this season, the females becomes extremely distended with eggs prior to laying them in a silky tangle on leaves and vegetation.

95 Ashy-grey Slug *Limax cinereoniger*
The ashy-grey slug is the largest of its kind in Britain, reaching a length of 140mm when fully extended; when contracted in alarm, it is the size of a golf ball. Ashy-grey slugs generally spend the daylight hours hidden beneath a fallen log where they can sometimes be found. During rainy or damp weather, however, they may venture forth in the day leaving a trail of silvery slime behind them. Ashy-grey slugs feed mainly on algae, mosses and seedlings, a rather restricted diet considering their large size. They are fairly common in New Forest woodlands, especially under beech trees.

96 Triops *Apus cancriformis*
Both in terms of its appearance and its life history, triops is one of the most unusual creatures to be found in the New Forest. Full-grown individuals may reach 4cm in length and resemble nothing so much as a miniature horseshoe crab. These primitive crustaceans are known from one or two winter-wet pools and hollows in the region. The tiny eggs, which are laid in their thousands, lie amongst the dried mud of the pond bottom during the summer months. It is only when autumn rain refreshes the pools that the eggs hatch. Triops is rare and protected. If you see one, admire it, but leave it in peace.

SHRUBS AND TREES

97 **Bog Myrtle** *Myrica gale* (H. 2m)
Bog myrtle is a deciduous shrub that forms fairly extensive patches on boggy heathland and beside streams in the New Forest. When walking through such an area, the plant announces itself with its heady, aromatic and resinous fragrance. This is stronger still if the leaves are rubbed and the smell does wonders for visitors with blocked sinuses or colds. Bog myrtle has brown twigs and oblong-ovate leaves that are rather tough. The plant produces reddish-brown male catkins and green, oval female catkins, with both sexes often appearing on the same plant.

98 **Silver Birch** *Betula pendula* (H. 25m)
Silver birch is the characteristic tree of heathland areas in the New Forest. It is quick to colonise and fast growing. Consequently, were it not controlled, it would eventually spread and form dense, impenetrable patches of scrub, thus eliminating the heath itself. Silver birch has drooping branches and bark which is reddish in young specimens but silvery-grey and peeling in mature trees. The leaves are rather triangular and toothed. In spring, they are bright green, while for a few days in autumn they turn golden-yellow, sometimes all at the same time.

99 **Scots Pine** *Pinus sylvestris* (H. 40m)
Although the Scots pine is not native to the New Forest, or indeed to southern England as a whole, it has successfully established itself having spread from plantations. Despite its alien origins, mature trees, as opposed to regimented plantation specimens, certainly do not look out of character on windswept heaths. The bark of Scots pine is reddish-brown and deeply cracked to form longitudinal plates. The needles grow in pairs and are twisted. The hanging cones may reach 60mm in length and eventually become oval in shape when mature.

100 **Pedunculate Oak** *Quercus robur* (H. 45m)
The pedunculate oak is the most likely species of oak to be found in the New Forest. The leaves have the typical shape on an oak and are borne on very short stalks. In the spring, the yellowish-green female and male catkins are produced separately. In the autumn, acorns, sitting in scaly cups, are carried on longish stalks. The acorns are an important source of food for woodland birds and mammals. The tree itself is also of immense importance in the woodland ecology of the New Forest, supporting more species of insect than any other tree in Britain.

101 **Ash** *Fraxinus excelsior* (H. 40m)
Although native to the New Forest, the ash is a comparatively unusual species. Because it stood out from other trees, it was often planted to mark the boundaries of woodlands as can be seen well at Mark Ash Wood near Bolderwood. A mature ash has a domed and rather open canopy. Its leaves are 25-30cm long and are divided into seven to 13 leaflets, each one of which is roughly oval with a toothed margin. In April and May, the tree produces sprays of purple flowers while, in the autumn, the familiar ash keys appear and are carried on the wind with a single wing.

A ROYAL HUNTING FOREST

At some point between the arrival of William the Conqueror in Britain in 1066, and the creation of the Domesday Book in 1086, the New Forest had become a royal hunting forest protected by the law.

The prime reason for its establishment was, of course, the protection of deer for hunting. However, the maintenance and exploitation of the forest was strictly controlled and restricted, as was settlement of the land.

Red deer stag.

103 **Beech** *Fagus sylvatica* (H. 40m)
In terms of colour, the beech is one of the most attractive trees in the New Forest. In the spring, the young leaves are a particularly bright and fresh green, darkening to deep green in the summer months. In the autumn, they change to golden-yellow or brown before falling, creating a colourful spectacle on sunny September days. Even in the winter, the tree still provides colour in the form of a carpet of rich brown leaves offset by silver-grey trunks. Beech leaves are oval, shiny and untoothed. The seeds — called 'mast' — provide a harvest for birds such as chaffinches and jays, as well as mice and squirrels.

104 **Holly** *Ilex aquifolium* (H. 10m)
Holly trees can be seen growing in a variety of settings in the New Forest, from open heathland to ancient woodland. It is an evergreen tree and stands out particularly well in the winter months when female trees often bear their characteristic red berries. These are a favourite food for birds such as thrushes and the seeds are dispersed in the birds' droppings. It is not coincidence, therefore, that holly trees often develop beneath overhanging branches of oaks and other trees, where birds frequently perch. Despite their prickly margins, holly leaves are eaten by deer and many trees show a browse line.

102 **Alder** *Alnus glutinosa* (H. 15m)
The alder is invariably found growing near water and, in the New Forest, often follows the courses of boggy streams along valley bottoms. In the summer months, it can be recognised by its rounded leaves which are 4-10cm long, widest above the middle and notched at the apex. From February to March, before the leaves are produced, catkins appear, the males of which resemble the catkins of trees such as hazel and willow. Female catkins are purplish and egg-shaped at first but become green as they fruit; when ripe, they are brown. They persist over the winter, the seeds providing food for siskins and redpolls.

WILDFLOWERS

105 Coral-necklace *Illecebrum verticillatum*
Coral-necklace is one of the plants that lures keen botanists to the New Forest, its only stronghold in Britain. Like many of the region's other specialities, it grows on boggy soils, often around the margins of ponds which flood in the winter. Coral-necklace is low-growing and trailing with reddish stems.
The leaves are oval and opposite with clusters of small, white flowers at their bases. Not surprisingly, the plant stands out well against the ground on which it is growing when in flower, and the name of coral-necklace appears extremely apt.

106 White Water-lily *Nymphaea alba*
With its large, floating leaves, which are 10-30cm in diameter, the white water-lily is an unmistakable plant.
It grows on many of the larger ponds and lakes in the New Forest and also on surprisingly small water bodies such as those around Hatchet Pond. The flowers are 10-20cm in diameter and have 20 or more petals which are white, often with a pinkish tinge. They open only in bright sunshine, remaining in tight buds at night and on dull days. By the end of the summer, white water-lily can form a blanket covering of the water where it grows. The undersides of the leaves are often covered with water snails and their eggs.

107 Marsh Marigold *Caltha palustris*
When you see marsh marigold in flower, you know that spring is not far away. As the name suggests, it favours damp habitats such as riversides and marshes, sometimes even growing in a few inches of water. Marsh marigold is fairly widespread in the New Forest in suitable habitats and is abundant in some of the damp woods around Beaulieu.
It flowers from May to July, the flowers resembling large, yellow buttercups up to 50mm in diameter. In actual fact, petals are absent, the colour being provided by yellow sepals. The leaves are distinctively heart- or kidney-shaped and up to 10cm across.

109 Round-leaved Sundew *Drosera rotundifolia*
Round-leaved sundew is the commonest of the three species of sundew that grow in the New Forest. All are unusual plants, supplementing their nutrient intake with an insectivorous diet. The rounded leaves are produced in a basal rosette. They are covered with glandular hairs, the tips of which exude a sticky liquid. Insects become trapped and enzymes in the liquid gradually digest them, nutrients being absorbed by the leaves. Round-leaved sundew produces flowering stalks from June to August, the flowers themselves being small, white, and opening only in bright sunlight.

110 Bramble *Rubus fruticosus*
Bramble is a typical plant of woodland rides, scrub and hedgerows. Well known for its scrambling and trailing appearance and coating of fierce prickles, it is perhaps best regarded for its fruits — blackberries — which are the delight of ramblers and woodland creatures alike. Bramble flowers from May to September, the blackberries ripening from late August onwards. Despite its invasive qualities, it is an important plant for many of the New Forest's animals, both small and large. In hard winters, it is eaten by deer and livestock and so seldom thrives in areas where they are numerous.

108 Pond Water-crowfoot *Ranunculus peltatus*
By late summer, some of the smaller ponds in the New Forest are covered with a carpet of leaves and studded with white flowers. The plant responsible for this dramatic transformation in the pond's appearance is likely to be pond water-crowfoot, a member of the buttercup family that always lives in water. Rather curiously, the plant has two types of leaves: on the surface, the floating leaves are somewhat shamrock-like but the submerged leaves, on the other hand, are finely divided and filamentous. The flowers have five petals and appear from May to August.

111 Tormentil *Potentilla erecta*
From spring to summer, grassy heathland tracks and woodland rides in the New Forest are studded with the bright yellow flowers of tormentil. The plant is perennial and has both creeping and ascending stems up to 25cm long. The unstalked leaves are trifoliate, the leaflets being slightly hairy underneath. The flowers are roughly 10mm in diameter and comprise four petals that are easily dislodged; they are carried on stalks 30mm in length. Tormentil flowers from May to August and is often common in suitable habitats.

112 Common Gorse *Ulex europaeus*
Although gorse can be found in flower at almost any time of year, it flowers mostly in the spring. In May and June, whole hillsides can turn bright yellow and the heady coconut smell of the flowers pervades the air. Common gorse forms dense evergreen shrubs, the twigs of which are extremely spiny. When growing *en masse*, it forms almost impenetrable cover for nesting birds such as Dartford warblers and stonechats. From the shape of the flowers, it is easy to see that common gorse is a member of the pea family. The seeds are produced in pods that burst explosively on hot summer days.

113 Dwarf Gorse *Ulex minor*
As its name suggests, dwarf gorse forms a much smaller shrub than the common gorse alongside which it grows. It is seldom more than 1m tall and often spreads among ling and bell heather. In many other respects, however, dwarf gorse is similar to its common relative. The individual flowers are much the same size and also produced in terminal spikes. It also bears spines but these are less rigid than those of common gorse. One of the best ways of identifying dwarf gorse is by its flowering period which lasts from July to September, much later in the season than common gorse.

114 Broom *Cytisus scoparius*

Broom is widespread and often quite common in the New Forest, being found in areas of scrub, open woodland and grassy areas. It forms dense shrubs which may reach up to 2m in height. The large and attractive yellow flowers appear from May to July and are arranged along the straight, spineless twigs. Broom leaves are trifoliate and are also arranged in groups along the twigs. Like common gorse, the flowers of broom are extremely popular with insects which collect pollen and nectar in abundance. The seed pods are oblong in shape and become black as they ripen.

115 Marsh St John's-wort *Hypericum elodes*

Marsh St John's-wort is extremely restricted in its choice of habitat, growing on boggy, peaty soil, often beside heathland streams and ponds. Where it does grow, however, it is often seen in profusion and may surround entire pools at a level where suitable soil conditions prevail. The oval, green leaves and stems are covered in greyish, silky hairs giving the plant a distinctive colour. The yellow flowers are 10-15mm across and are produced in small clusters on upright stems. They do not open widely and close on dull days and late in the afternoon.

116 Common Dog-violet *Viola riviniana*

Woodland rides and grassy roadside verges are typical habitats for the common dog-violet, one of several similar species to be found in the New Forest. The flowers, typically violet-like in appearance, are produced from March to May and small clumps can be seen in good locations. They are carried on leafy stalks which arise from a basal clump of leaves. The individual flowers are 20mm across and bluish-violet in colour with darker lines converging on the centre. The leaves are more or less heart-shaped, roughly 35mm across and hairless on long stalks.

117 Hampshire-purslane *Ludwigia palustris*

As its name suggests, Hampshire-purslane is more or less confined to Hampshire in its British range, with the boundaries of the New Forest effectively defining its distribution in the county. It is a wetland plant, growing around the muddy margins of pools and ponds; in suitable habitats it can be quite common. Hampshire-purslane is a creeping perennial, with reddish stems up to 55cm in length. The oval leaves are produced in opposite pairs along the stem and the curious flowers, comprising a tubular arrangement of sepals, are seen in the leaf axils. Hampshire-purslane flowers from June to August.

115

117

If left to follow the course of nature, mature trees eventually begin to decay, the unstable trunk eventually collapsing.

With careful management, the life of an oak can be extended beyond the usual 300-400 years. Some of the largest and most stately oaks, such as the Knightwood Oak, are thought to be more than 600 years old and have been pollarded on a regular basis for much of their lives.

The Knightwood Oak.

117A Ling *Calluna vulgaris*

An expanse of New Forest heath in full bloom is a memorable sight. Visit the area in July and August and you will find vast tracts of heathland covered in flowering ling, the commonest and most widespread member of the heather family in southern England. The individual flowers are mostly pinkish, but sometimes white forms occur. They are only about 4mm long but large numbers are produced on each spike. The leaves, small, hairless and rather tough and leathery, are arranged in four rows along the stems and remain throughout the year.

118 Bell Heather *Erica cinerea*

Bell heather is a distinctive relative of ling with which it is often found growing. It forms sizeable clumps, up to 50cm high, on dry heathland soils. The flowers are usually deep purple in colour, bell-like in appearance and arranged in loose groups near the top of upright stems. The leaves are rather spiky and are produced in threes but arranged in whorls on the stems. Bell heather flowers from June to September. It is usually found growing within larger areas of ling, but in favourable conditions it can cover quite extensive areas.

119 Cross-leaved Heath *Erica tetralix*

Cross-leaved heath is never as common as the other two heather species found in the New Forest. It favours damper situations and is entirely characteristic of boggy valley bottoms, often with sphagnum moss growing in the vicinity. Cross-leaved heath is less robust than its relatives, seldom reaching more than 20cm in height. As its name suggests, the spiky leaves are arranged in fours up the stems. The flowers are extremely distinctive, being pale pink in colour, 7mm long and arranged in tight clusters at the ends of the stems.

120 Bilberry *Vaccinium myrtillus*
Woodland rides on acid soils and heathlands are favoured habitats for bilberry, which is also known as whortleberry. Where grazing pressure is not too great, it forms low, straggly clumps, and sometimes almost continuous cover. The stems are bright green and triple-angled, and bear finely-toothed, oval leaves that are also bright green. The flowers are reddish and lantern-shaped; they are solitary and seen from April to June. The subsequent berries are bluish-black but covered with a greyish dusting that easily rubs off. Bilberries, found during the summer months, are delicious to eat.

121 Bog Pimpernel *Anagallis tenella*
On sunny days from June to August, heathland boggy flushes in the New Forest are often studded with the delightful pink flowers of bog pimpernel. The plant itself is a hairless, creeping perennial with slender stems carrying pairs of elliptical or rounded leaves. The funnel-shaped flowers are 10mm long and divided into five lobes. The pink petals are scored with darker veins and the flowers close during dull weather. Bog pimpernel is widespread in the Forest and forms extensive carpets in some areas, often growing on sphagnum moss.

122 Bogbean *Menyanthes trifoliata*
Bogbean is often seen growing in the shallow water of heathland pools but also favours damp, boggy areas if the ground is really waterlogged. The attractive white flowers are carried in dense, upright spikes with the individual star-like flowers comprising five petals with a fringe of white hairs. The plant's name derives from the appearance of its leaves which look, and feel, like those of a broad-bean. Bogbean is a perennial plant with a creeping rhizome. It flowers from April to June and is locally fairly common in suitable habitats in the New Forest.

125 Foxglove *Digitalis purpurea*
The foxglove is one of the most distinctive plants in the New Forest. It thrives on acid soils and is often seen in woodland clearings and on roadside verges and heaths. Tall flowering spikes of foxgloves appear from May to August, with a succession of individual flowers appearing as the spike lengthens. The flowers are tubular and drooping but the opening is sufficiently broad to allow pollinating insects such as bumblebees to land. The leaves are broadly oval with a downy upper surface. A rosette of leaves persists for a year from which the flower spike grows in the following spring.

126 Lousewort *Pedicularis sylvatica*
The presence of lousewort is often indicative of poor grazing because the plant does best on heaths, bogs and nutrient-poor grassy areas. The attractive pink flowers are a distinctive shape with a long, curved upper lip and flattened lower lip. They are produced from a pale green calyx, which soon becomes inflated, and are carried in terminal clusters of five or more flowers. The leaves of lousewort are finely divided and rather feathery, although tough in texture. Lousewort flowers from April to July but the plant itself is perennial.

123 Marsh Gentian *Gentiana pneumonanthe*
Because of loss of habitat, marsh gentian is an extremely scarce plant in Britain as a whole. It is, however, locally common on a few areas of grassy heath in the New Forest. Its attractive, blue flowers appear in August and September and are 25-35mm long and bell-shaped. They are carried in terminal clusters of up to six flowers, the plant itself often growing from a clump of purple moor-grass. The leaves are narrow, blunt-tipped and carried up the stem. Without the flowers, this perennial plant is very difficult to locate in its grassy habitat.

124 Narrow-leaved Lungwort *Pulmonaria longifolia*
The New Forest is the main stronghold in Britain for the narrow-leaved lungwort, so-called because of the appearance of its pale-spotted leaves which fancifully resemble lungs; early herbalists used the plant to treat breathing disorders and consumption. The attractive flowers appear in clusters during April and May. Initially pinkish-red in colour, they soon turn bluish-purple. Narrow-leaved lungwort is affected by grazing pressure in the New Forest and usually thrives only where this is restricted by, for example, the proximity of a road or an inclosure fence.

127 Honeysuckle *Lonicera periclymenum*
Sometimes mistakenly taken for a parasite, honeysuckle is a sprawling, climbing shrub that uses trees for support rather than nutrients. In shady woodlands it is often rather straggly, while in open, sunny areas its growth is more lush. The oval leaves are carried in opposite pairs on the twining stems which can reach 5m in length. The elongated flowers are produced from June to September in terminal whorls. They are heavily scented and are particularly attractive to night-feeding moths. The juicy red berries are popular with mice and birds alike.

128 Small Fleabane *Pulicaria vulgaris*
Although small fleabane is not the most showy of plants, it certainly causes great interest among keen botanists visiting the New Forest. The region is by far the most important stronghold for this species in Britain, which depends on rather unusual habitat requirements for its survival. Small fleabane prefers winter-wet hollows where the competing vegetation is kept down, so areas of constant grazing around ditches and dried pond margins are the places to look. The flower heads are 10mm across and dull yellow in colour; the plant itself is much branched.

129 Ragwort *Senecio jacobaea*
Ragwort is the bane of anyone who keeps
a pony in the New Forest. Clumps of this
vigorous and invasive plant thrive on
wasteground and grazed land but all parts
are poisonous to livestock. Were it not for
its unpopularity, it would be considered an
attractive plant with its dense heads of
yellow daisy-like flowers carried on tall,
leafy stems. Ragwort flowers from June
to September but the basal leaf stock is
often perennial. During the summer
months, the plant is sometimes covered
with the orange and black, stripy
caterpillars of the cinnabar moth.

130 Bog Asphodel
Narthecium ossifragum
During the months of June, July and
August, many of the New Forest's boggy
valleys and heathland flushes are adorned
with the striking yellow flowers of bog
asphodel. Often abundant in suitable
locations, the plant is one of the most
colourful members of the heathland flora.
The individual flowers are star shaped,
12mm in diameter and show bright
orange-red filaments. They are carried on
upright spikes which may be up to 12cm
tall. The leaves are spiky and tough;
together with the fruits, they turn orange-
brown by late summer.

131 Wild Gladiolus *Gladiolus illyricus*
The New Forest is the only place in Britain
where the wild gladiolus is found; here it is
locally common but invariably difficult to
find. The flowers are among the most
striking and attractive of any plant in the
region. They are a typical gladiolus shape,
pinkish-purple in colour and carried on tall
spikes of three to nine flowers. The leaves
are long, thin and extremely grass-like.
Non-flowering plants, which often
predominate, are consequently very
difficult to locate in the grassy habitats
where the plant grows. Wild gladiolus is
often found under bracken in woodland
rides and on wooded heaths.

132 Bog Orchid *Hammarbya paludosa*
As its name suggests, the tiny bog orchid
is a plant of heathland bogs and wet
flushes, often growing in the very wettest
locations where sphagnum moss forms a
floating bog. The miniature orchid flowers
are carried on an upright spike, 8-10cm
in height. Like the rest of the plant they are
yellowish-green and distinctively brighter
than the vegetation with which they are
found growing. At the base of the flowering
spike there are three or four rounded or
oval leaves, sometimes partly hidden
among mosses. Bog orchid flowers from
July to September.

130

131

Small herds of these rugged ponies can be seen throughout the New Forest except where inclosure fences deliberately exclude them.

Now a recognised breed, the New Forest pony has been here for many centuries and originally derives from Welsh bloodstock with subsequent introductions of Highland, Exmoor, Dartmoor and other ponies. Every year, large numbers are rounded up and taken to horse stalls at Beaulieu Road Station, where they are marked or sold. New Forest ponies make excellent riding horses, being sure-footed and obedient. Not surprisingly, they are popular with local inhabitants and riding schools.

133 Heath Spotted-orchid *Dactylorhiza maculata*
The heath spotted-orchid is the most conspicuous and characteristic orchid to be found on drier areas of heath in the New Forest. Its pale flowers are carried on fairly dense spikes which are slightly pyramidal in outline, especially in their early stages. The individual flowers are pale pink with darker spotting and streaking on the lower lip. The leaves are long and narrow, and are marked with dark spots; this characteristic is useful in identifying the plant before the flowers have appeared. Heath spotted-orchid flowers from May to early August.

134 Common Cotton-grass *Eriophorum angustifolium*
Many areas of the New Forest are treacherously boggy and a good indication of the wettest of these is the presence of common cotton-grass. Scan an area like Beaulieu Road Station or Denny Bog and you will see hundreds of cotton-like tassels blowing in the wind. The flowers of common cotton-grass are relatively insignificant. It is not until after flowering that the silky, white hairs develop, a tuft being attached to each seed or 'spikelet'; the hairs eventually assist in their wind dispersal. Common cotton-grass flowers from April to July, the cotton-like heads persisting longer.

135 Purple Moor-grass *Molinia caerulea*
Purple moor-grass is a characteristic and distinctive plant of wet heaths, bogs and, more occasionally, heathy woodland rides in the New Forest. It prefers areas that are waterlogged at least in the winter months and often grows with cross-leaved heath. Purple moor-grass gets its name from the purple flower heads. It is a tussock-forming plant that is perennial, the tough and wiry leaves and stems persisting throughout the winter. Tussocks of the grass are often covered with spiders' webs in autumn which, with a coating of hoar frost, make a memorable sight in the morning light.

136 Bracken *Pteridium aquilinum*

There can be few areas in the New Forest where a visitor can stand and not see bracken. It is by far the most abundant and widespread fern in the region and one of the commonest of all plants. Bracken dies back in the winter months but in the spring, new shoots appear, the leafy tips curled at first. The expanded fronds are bright green but darken with age. Very few creatures eat bracken and so the fronds remain more or less intact. By September, the bracken has begun to change colour and whole hillsides sometimes turn golden-brown or yellow.

137 Polypody Fern *Polypodium vulgare*

Grazing pressure from ponies and deer is intense in the New Forest. As a consequence, ferns that might otherwise be found at ground level are often restricted to inaccessible sites. Although sometimes found on banks or walls, polypody characteristically occurs on branches of trees, growing among the mosses and lichens. Sites where the fern does thrive are always damp and shady, the humidity offsetting the problems these lower plants have with water loss. Polypody fern has rather oblong fronds, with broad, rounded-tipped lobes.

138 Sphagnum Moss *Sphagnum auriculatum*

Sphagnum moss is typical of boggy habitats in the New Forest. However, on close inspection you will see that there is considerable variation in its appearance and keen botanists separate the group into several species. The one illustrated here is typical of open bogs and sometimes forms bright green patches rather like miniature lawns. Walkers would be ill-advised to walk on these, however, since the moss sometimes grows out over open water, forming a thin crust — a so-called blanket bog. Leafy spikes of sphagnum grow closely packed so that the terminal rosettes are often all that can be seen.

139 White Fork Moss *Leucobryum glaucum*
This is one of the most distinctive mosses to be found in the New Forest. It is characteristic of grazed woodlands and forms grey-green cushions which may be up to 15cm in diameter. These cushions comprise densely packed, narrow leaves which become almost white when dry. Being only loosely attached to the soil, the moss cushions easily become detached, rolled around and broken. Visitors should refrain from the temptation to dislodge or collect this rather fragile species. White fork moss persists throughout the year.

140 *Cladonia floerkeana*
Cladonia floerkeana is one of many species of lichens that grow on heathland in the New Forest. It is found at ground level, often in and around the stems of ling and bell heather or on bare patches of gravelly soil. Most of the body of the lichen is tough and grey-green in colour, with a rather powdery or granular surface texture. It does, however, have very distinctive spore-producing bodies on the ends of upright stalks, 10mm high. These are bright red and earn this, and other similar species, the nickname of 'pixie's caps'.

FUNGI

141 Fly Agaric *Amanita muscaria*

During September and October, the distinctive and poisonous fly agaric is a common sight in open, birch woodlands in the New Forest. This is the archetypal toadstool that features in so many children's books and the species is difficult to confuse with any other. Fly agarics form an underground association with birch roots and the toadstool itself is the fruiting body of the fungus. The cap is bright red, up to 10cm in diameter and covered in white, scaly flecks that get washed off in the rain. The white stem arises from a swollen base and may stand 15cm high.

142 Birch Polypore *Piptoporus betulinus*

The birch polypore is a bracket fungus which, as the name suggests, is found on birch trees. It grows on the trunks and, in mature specimens, the bracket may be 15 or 20cm across. The upper surface is pale brown or fawn in colour and may be rather speckled or blotched. The lower surface is covered with tiny white pores from which the spores are produced. The bracket may be up to 5cm thick near the base; it is firmly attached to the birch trunk on which it grows and is very tough. In the past, dried birch polypores were used by country folk for sharpening razors.

143 *Ramaria stricta*

Walk through a mature conifer plantation in the autumn, and you are sure to find a wealth of different fungi. *Ramaria stricta* is one of the most unusual and attractive of these and can be seen from late September to November, growing on fallen twigs among the carpet of pine needles. It grows to a height of 10cm and is extremely branched, resembling a miniature tree, or perhaps one of the more bizarre corals. *Ramaria stricta* is usually buffish-cinnamon in colour although it may appear rather bleached later in the season. Although it is not poisonous, it is tough and inedible.

141

143

142

144 Cep *Boletus edulis*

Also known as the 'penny bun', the cep is beloved of gastronomes on account of its rich flavour. It is fairly common in the New Forest although it suffers from over-collecting and is often confused with other similar species of fungi.

The cep has a rounded, brown cap that may reach 10cm in diameter and is thick and fleshy. On the under surface there are pale yellowish pores from which the spores are released.

The stem is thick and bulbous at the base. Ceps are soon attacked by insects such as fly larvae and the caps and stems are often riddled with holes.

145 Shaggy Ink-cap *Coprinus comatus*

Small troops of shaggy ink-caps are a common sight along roadside verges and on grassy woodland rides in the New Forest. They appear during September and October and fungi at different stages of development often grow side by side.

In its early stages, the shaggy ink-cap has a pale, rather egg-shaped cap which appears almost to enclose the stem. After a day or so, the stem elongates, reaching a height of 15cm, and the cap expands. Finally the gills liquefy, the spores being spread by rain. In its young stages, the shaggy ink-cap is edible and delicious.

146 Parasol Mushroom *Lepiota procera*

The parasol mushroom is a large and distinctive fungus. It grows in grassland and, in the New Forest, is sometimes seen on roadside verges or grazed grassy areas. Where you find one, you will usually find several and they may form fairly large groups. As its name suggests, a mature parasol mushroom has a superficial resemblance to an umbrella. The cap is broad and flattened and sometimes more than 20cm in diameter; it is buffish in colour but covered in darker brown scales. The stem may be 30cm in length and is covered in fine scales, often arranged in rings.

147 Hairy Stereum *Stereum hirsutum*

In the New Forest, fallen trees and branches are often left where they lie to decay and return their nutrients to the soil. Essential in the process of decay is the action of fungi, and tree stumps are often covered with a bewildering range of bracket-like species. One of the most distinctive of these is the hairy stereum which has 2cm-wide brackets often arranged in rows and tiers on the surface of the wood. The colour is rather variable although the fungus is frequently bright yellow. The upper surface is always covered in a layer of hairs, a feature which aids identification.

148 Common Earth-ball *Scleroderma citrinum*

The woodland floor is the place to search for the common earth-ball. This curious species is fairly common in the New Forest and begins to appear in September, especially after heavy rain. At first, the earth-ball resembles an old tennis ball in size and shape, the surface being covered in brown scales; it can be rather difficult to spot among the fallen leaves. As the earth-ball matures, the surface splits and cracks, revealing a yellow inner layer and finally the black mass of spores. These are washed out by the rain during autumn downpours.

149 Sulphur Tuft *Hypholoma fasciculare*

Sulphur tuft is an extremely good name for this species which is sulphury-yellow in colour and does indeed grow in tufts or clumps. It is invariably found growing on dead wood such as tree stumps, although the wood itself may occasionally be buried in the soil; broad-leaved trees rather than conifers are preferred. The individual fungi have caps up to 3cm in diameter and these are carried on curved or distorted stems up to 6cm in length. Sulphur tufts appear in the autumn. Even if killed off by severe frosts they may regrow when milder weather returns.

THE BEAULIEU RIVER

From its source in the heart of the New Forest near Lyndhurst, the Beaulieu River makes its way gently to the Solent.

Along its course it passes through areas of heathland and woodland before it finally broadens and becomes tidal. Walks along the river bank at Bucklers Hard are good for birdwatching, especially during the winter months. Keep an eye open particularly for waders such as redshank and dunlin as well as wildfowl such as Brent geese and wigeon. At the mouth of the river lies Needs Ore Point, managed as a reserve by English Nature. Occasional boat trips allow visitors to see the tens of thousands of birds that breed here; these include black-headed gulls, Sandwich, common and little terns and shelduck.

Dunlin, a typical wader.

PLACES OF INTEREST

The following places of interest lie within the New Forest area and can be located on the map on pages 4 and 5.

• Beaulieu National Motor Museum

Beaulieu. Tel: 01590 612345.
A collection of over 250 vehicles dating from the late 19th century to the present day with various transport-related displays and motoring memorabilia. A monorail, veteran buses and a model railway take visitors round the grounds.
Open daily all year except Christmas Day.

• Braemore House

Braemore. Tel: 01725 512468.
Fine 16th century country house with a countryside museum showing trades and crafts of the past. The stables house a collection of horse-drawn vehicles.
Open Easter, Bank Holidays, and April to September from 2-5.30pm inclusive on varying days.

• Buckler's Hard Maritime Museum

Buckler's Hard. Tel: 01590 616203.
Ships for Nelson's fleet were built at Buckler's Hard and the museum recalls the local life and industries of that time.
Open daily all year except Christmas Day.

• Exbury Gardens

Exbury. Tel: 01703 891203.
Over 200 acres of landscaped woodland gardens, on the Beaulieu River. Rhododendrons, azaleas, camellias and magnolias a speciality. Cafe, plant centre and gift shop.
Gardens open mid-March to October at varying times. Plant centre and gift shop open daily, except Christmas Day and Boxing Day.

• Furzey Gardens

Minstead. Tel: 01703 812464.
Eight acres of gardens with year-round interest surround a cottage where local arts and crafts can be seen.
Open daily all year except Christmas Day.

• Lepe Country Park

Lepe. Tel: 01962 846034.
A country park overlooking the Solent with a long stretch of beach. Grassy area, picnic site, children's playground and cafe.
Open at all times.

• New Forest Butterfly Farm

Longdown, Ashhurst. Tel: 01703 292166.
Butterflies and moths from all over the world live in a giant indoor jungle here. An outdoor area has been designed to attract dragonflies.
Open daily early April to end October.

• New Forest Museum and Visitor Centre

Main Car Park, Lyndhurst. Tel: 01703 283914.
All aspects of the Forest's history can be discovered here — traditions, organisations and wildlife. Gift shop and tourist information centre here too.
Open daily all year except Christmas Day.

USEFUL ADDRESSES

- **Countryside Commission**
  John Dower House
  Crescent Place
  Cheltenham, Glos GL50 3RA

- **English Nature (Headquarters)**
  Northminster House
  Peterborough, PE1 1UA

- **Forestry Commission (Regional Office)**
  Avon Fields House
  Somerdale
  Keynsham
  Bristol BS18 2BD

- **Hampshire County Council**
  Recreation Dept
  North Hill Close
  Andover Road
  Winchester, Hants SO22 6AQ

- **Hampshire and Isle of Wight Naturalists' Trust**
  8 Market Place
  Romsey, Hants SO5 8NB

- **National Trust (Regional Office)**
  Polesden Lacey
  Dorking, Surrey RH5 6BD

- **RSPB (Headquarters)**
  The Lodge
  Sandy, Beds SG19 2DL

- **Wildfowl Trust**
  Slimbridge
  Glos GL2 7BT

INDEX